T0058981

SCHIRMER'S LIBRARY
OF MUSICAL CLASSICS

FREDERIC CHOPIN
Complete Works for the Piano

Edited and Fingered,
and provided with an Introductory Note by
CARL MIKULI

Historical and Analytical Comments by
JAMES HUNEKER

ISBN 978-0-7935-5704-2

G. SCHIRMER, Inc.

DISTRIBUTED BY

HAL•LEONARD®
CORPORATION
7777 W. BLUEMOUND RD. P.O. BOX 13819 MILWAUKEE, WI 53213

FRÉDÉRIC FRANÇOIS CHOPIN

According to a tradition—and, be it said, an erroneous one—Chopin's playing was like that of one dreaming rather than awake—scarcely audible in its continual *pianissimos* and *una cordas*, with feebly developed technique and quite lacking in confidence, or at least indistinct, and distorted out of all rhythmic form by an incessant *tempo rubato!* The effect of these notions could not be otherwise than very prejudicial to the interpretation of his works, even by the most able artists—in their very striving after truthfulness; besides, they are easily accounted for.

Chopin played rarely and always unwillingly in public; "exhibitions" of himself were totally repugnant to his nature. Long years of sickliness and nervous irritability did not always permit him the necessary repose, in the concert-hall, for displaying untrammeled the full wealth of his resources. In more familiar circles, too, he seldom played anything but his shorter pieces, or occasional fragments from the larger works. Small wonder, therefore, that Chopin the Pianist should fail of general recognition.

Yet Chopin possessed a highly developed technique, giving him complete mastery over the instrument. In all styles of touch the evenness of his scales and passages was unsurpassed—nay, fabulous; under his hands the pianoforte needed to envy neither the violin for its bow nor wind-instruments for the living breath. The tones melted one into the other with the liquid effect of beautiful song.

A genuine piano-hand, extremely flexible though not large, enabled him to play arpeggios of most widely dispersed harmonies and passages in wide stretches, which he brought into vogue as something never attempted before; and everything without the slightest apparent exertion, a pleasing freedom and lightness being a distinguishing characteristic of his style. At the same time, the tone which he could *draw out* of the instrument was prodigious, especially in the *cantabiles;* in this regard John Field alone could compare with him.

A lofty, virile energy lent imposing effect to suitable passages—an energy without roughness; on the other hand, he could carry away his hearers by the tenderness of his soulful delivery—a tenderness without affectation. But with all the warmth of his peculiarly ardent temperament, his playing was always within bounds, chaste, polished and at times even severely reserved.

In keeping time Chopin was inflexible, and many will be surprised to learn that the metronome never left his piano. Even in his oft-decried *tempo rubato* one hand—that having the accompaniment—always played on in strict time, while the other, singing the melody, either hesitating as if undecided, or, with increased animation, anticipating with a kind of impatient vehemence as if in passionate utterances, maintained the freedom of musical expression from the fetters of strict regularity.

Some information concerning Chopin the Teacher, even in the shape of a mere sketch, can hardly fail to interest many readers.

Far from regarding his work as a teacher, which his position as an artist and his social connections in Paris rendered difficult of avoidance, as a burdensome task, Chopin daily devoted his entire energies to it for several hours and with genuine delight. True, his demands on the talent and industry of the pupil were very great. There were often "de leçons orageuses" ("stormy lessons"), as they were called in school parlance, and many a fair eye wet with tears departed from the high altar of the Cité d'Orleans, rue St. Lazare, yet without the slightest resentment on that score against the dearly beloved master. For this same severity, so little prone to easy satisfaction, this feverish vehemence with which the master strove to raise his disciples to his own plane, this insistence on the repetition of a passage until it was understood, were a guaranty that he had the pupil's progress at heart. He would glow with a sacred zeal for art; every word from his lips was stimulating and inspiring. Single lessons often lasted literally for several hours in succession, until master and pupil were overcome by fatigue.

On beginning with a pupil, Chopin was chiefly anxious to do away with any stiffness in, or cramped, convulsive movement of, the hand, thereby obtaining the first requisite of a fine technique, "souplesse" (suppleness), and at the same time independence in the motion of the fingers. He was never tired of inculcating that such technical exercises are not merely mechanical, but claim the intelligence and entire will-power of the pupil; and, consequently, that a twentyfold or fortyfold repetition (still the lauded arcanum of so many schools) does no good whatever—not to mention the kind of practising advocated by Kalkbrenner, during which one may also occupy oneself with reading! He treated the various styles of touch very thoroughly, more especially the full-toned *legato.*

As gymnastic aids he recommended bending the wrist inward and outward, the repeated wrist-stroke, the pressing apart of the fingers—but all with an earnest warning against over-exertion. For scale-practice he required a very full tone, as *legato* as possible, at first very slowly and taking a quicker tempo only step by step, and playing with metronomic evenness. To facilitate the passing under of the thumb and passing over of the fingers the hand was to be bent inward. The scales having many black keys (B major, F-sharp, D-flat) were studied first, C major, as the hardest, coming last. In like order he took up Clementi's Preludes and Exercises, a work which he highly valued on account of its utility. According to Chopin, evenness in scale-playing and arpeggios depends not only on the equality in the strength of the fingers obtained through five-finger exercises, and a perfect freedom of the thumb in passing under and over, but foremostly on the perfectly smooth and constant sideways movement of the hand (not *step* by *step*), letting the elbow hang down freely and loosely at all times. This movement he exemplified by a *glissando* across the keys. After this he gave as studies a selection from Cramer's Études, Clementi's Gradus ad Parnassum, The Finishing Studies in Style by Moscheles, which were very congenial to him, Bach's English and French Suites, and some Preludes and Fugues from the Well-Tempered Clavichord.

Field's and his own nocturnes also figured to a certain extent as studies, for through them—partly by learning from his explanations, partly by hearing and imitating them as played indefatigably by Chopin himself—the pupil was taught to recognize, love and produce the *legato* and the beautiful connected singing tone. For paired notes and chords he exacted strictly simultaneous striking of the notes, an arpeggio being permitted only where marked by the composer himself; in the trill, which he generally commenced on the auxiliary, he required perfect evenness rather than great rapidity, the closing turn to be played easily and without haste.

For the turn (*gruppetto*) and appoggiatura he recommended the great Italian singers as models; he desired octaves to be played with the wrist-stroke, but without losing in fullness of tone thereby. Only far-advanced pupils were given his Études Op. 10 and Op. 25.

Chopin's attention was always directed to teaching correct phrasing. With reference to wrong phrasing he often repeated the apt remark, that it struck him as if some one were reciting, in a language not understood by the speaker, a speech carefully learned by rote, in the course of which the speaker not only neglected the natural quantity of the syllables, but even stopped in the middle of words. The pseudo-musician, he said, shows in a similar way, by his wrong phrasing, that music is not his mother-tongue, but something foreign and incomprehensible to him, and must, like the aforesaid speaker, quite renounce the idea of making any effect upon his hearers by his delivery.

In marking the fingering, especially that peculiar to himself, Chopin was not sparing. Piano-playing owes him many innovations in this respect, whose practicalness caused their speedy adoption, though at first certain authorities, like Kalkbrenner, were fairly horrified by them. For example, Chopin did not hesitate to use the thumb on the black keys, or to pass it under the little finger (with a decided inward bend of the wrist, to be sure), where it facilitated the execution, rendering the latter quieter and smoother. With one and the same finger he often struck two neighboring keys in succession (and this not simply in a slide from a black key to the next white one), without the slightest noticeable break in the continuity of the tones. He frequently passed the longest fingers over each other without the intervention of the thumb (see Étude No. 2, Op. 10), and not only in passages where (e.g.) it was made necessary by the holding down of a key with the thumb. The fingering for chromatic thirds based on this device (and marked by himself in Étude No. 5, Op. 25), renders it far easier to obtain the smoothest *legato* in the most rapid tempo, and with a perfectly quiet hand, than the fingering followed before. The fingerings in the present edition are, in most cases, those indicated by Chopin himself; where this is not the case, they are at least marked in conformity with his principles, and therefore calculated to facilitate the execution in accordance with his conceptions.

In the shading he insisted on a real and carefully graduated *crescendo* and *decrescendo*. On phrasing, and on style in general, he gave his pupils invaluable and highly suggestive hints and instructions, assuring himself, however, that they were understood by playing not only single passages, but whole pieces, over and over again, and this with a scrupulous care, an enthusiasm, such as none of his auditors in the concert-hall ever had an opportunity to witness. The whole lesson-hour often passed without the pupil's having played more than a few measures, while Chopin, at a Pleyel upright piano (the pupil always played on a fine concert grand, and was obliged to promise to practise on only the best instruments), continually interrupting and correcting, proffered for his admiration and imitation the warm, living ideal of perfect beauty. It may be asserted, without exaggeration, that only the pupil knew Chopin the Pianist in his entire unrivalled greatness.

Chopin most urgently recommended ensemble-playing, the cultivation of the best chamber-music—but only in association with the finest musicians. In case no such opportunity offered, the best substitute would be found in four-hand playing.

With equal insistence he advised his pupils to take up thorough theoretical studies as early as practicable. Whatever their condition in life, the master's great heart always beat warmly for the pupils. A sympathetic, fatherly friend, he inspired them to unwearying endeavor, took unaffected delight in their progress, and at all times had an encouraging word for the wavering and dispirited.

CARL MIKULI.

THE IMPROMPTUS

THE first Chopin Impromptu was published December, 1837; the second, May, 1840; the third, February, 1843; the Fantaisie-Impromptu, 66, was published by Fontana in 1855; it was opus composed about 1834. At least two of these Impromptus are almost denied us because of their eternal iteration; the Fantaisie-Impromptu and the one in A flat, seldom played beautifully, have become commonplaces. A greater Chopin is in the F sharp major Impromptu. It possesses the true impromptu spirit, the wandering, vagrant moods, the restless outpouring of fancy. The G flat is practically neglected; nevertheless, it is charming.

To write of the four Impromptus in their own key of unrestrained feeling, yet pondered intention, would be as difficult as recapturing the first careless rapture of the lark. With all the freedom of an improvisation the Chopin Impromptu has a well-defined form. There is a structural sense, though the pattern is free and original. The mood-color is not much varied in the first, third and fourth, but in the second there is a Ballade-like quality that hints at the tragic. The A flat Impromptu, opus 29, is, if one is pinned down to the title, the happiest named of the set. Its prankish, nimble, bubbling style is indicated from the start. The D natural in the treble against the C in the bass was once an original effect, while the flowing triplets of the first part lend a ductile, gracious, high-bred character. The chromatic involutions are many and interesting. When the F minor section is reached, the ear experiences the relief of a strongly contrasted rhythm. The simple duple measure, so naturally ornamented, is broadly melodious. After the return of the first theme there is a *coda*, and with a few chords in which *chiaroscuro* is suggested the composition rests. *Rubato* should be employed, for, as Kleczynski says: "Here everything totters from foundation to summit, and nevertheless, everything is so clear, so beautiful."

There is more pure grace of line and *limpidezza* in this first Impromptu than in the second, opus 36, in F sharp major. Here symmetry is abandoned, but compensation is offered because of intenser emotional issues. There is something sphinx-like in this work. Its nocturnal beginning with the carillon bass—the sunken bell!—the sweet-grave close of the episode, the faint hoof-beats of an approaching cavalcade, with the swelling thunder of its passage, surely suggest a narrative, a programme. After the D major picture there are two bars of anonymous modulation as "modern" as Schoenberg— these bars creak on their hinges—and the first

subject reappears in F, climbs to F sharp, thence merges into a melodic, glittering organ-point, with brilliant scale-passages, the whole subsiding into an echo of earlier harmonies. The final octaves are usually marked *fortissimo*, which always seems brutal. Yet its logic may lie imbedded in the scheme of the composer. Perhaps he wished to harshly arouse us from dreamland—as was his habit when improvising for friends; a *glissando* or a crashing chord would send them home shivering after an evening of delicious reverie. Niecks finds this Impromptu lacking the pith of the first, but for me it is of more moment than the other three. In outline it is as irregular and wavering, the moods errant and capricious, yet it would be bold to deny its power, its beauty. In its use of accessory figures it does not reveal much ingenuity, but just because the "figure in the carpet" is not so varied in pattern its passion is all the deeper. It is a species of Ballade, sadder, more meditative of the tender grace of a vanished day.

The third Impromptu in G flat, opus 51, is not often played. It may be too difficult for the student with an average technique, yet one hardly ventures to maintain that it is as fresh in feeling, as spontaneous in utterance, as its companions. There are touches of the *blasé*, of the jaded, the *rococo*, and in sentiment it is hardly profound. There are snake-like curves in triplets, as in the first Impromptu; but with interludes of double-notes, in coloring tropical and rich to morbidity. The E flat minor trio is a fine bit of melodic writing. The absence of simplicity is counterbalanced by greater freedom in modulation and complexity of pattern. But the Impromptu flavor is not missing, and there is allied to delicacy of design a strangeness, which Edgar Poe has declared should be a constituent of all great art. Opus 66 is a true Impromptu, although the prefix of Fantaisie given it by Fontana is superfluous. The piece presents some difficulties, chiefly of the rhythmic order. Its involuted first phrases suggest the Bellinian *coloratura* so dear to Chopin, but the D flat part is without nobility. Here is the same sort of saccharine melody that makes mawkish the trio of the Funeral March. There seems no fear that the Fantaisie-Impromptu will suffer from neglect, as it is the joy of the amateur, who usually transforms its *presto* into a slow, blurred mass of badly related rhythms and its slower episode into a long-drawn, sentimental agony. But in the hands of an adept pianist the C sharp minor Impromptu is of a charm, though **not of great depth.**

George Mathias once sketched Chopin for me in a few sincere strokes. His alluring, hesitating, gracious, feminine manner, coupled with his air of supreme distinction, were very attractive. M. Mathias—dear, old, charming gentleman, how well I remember him during the year 1878 at Paris—spoke to me of Chopin's way of holding his shoulders high, after the Polish style. Chopin often met Kalkbrenner, his antipodes in everything but breeding. Chopin's coat was buttoned close and high, the buttons black; those of Kalkbrenner were of gold. How Chopin disliked the pompous old pianist with his affected airs and his stinginess! Mathias was gleeful when he spoke of Kalkbrenner's offer to teach the Pole. "I believe it was Kalkbrenner who needed lessons from Chopin," he said. At Louis Viardot's Chopin met Thalberg; and that master of the arpeggio, and also of one of the finest singing touches ever heard on a keyboard, received with feigned humility the compliments of the Polish pianist, not altogether believing in their sincerity. Perhaps he was right, as Chopin mocked his mechanical style when his back was turned, his imitation of the old-fashioned "Moses in Egypt" fantaisie being very funny, according to Mathias. It must be remembered that Chopin, with all his Slavic poetry, his melancholy, and rather haughty bearing, was an astounding mimic and on his happy days full of fun and tricks. Bocage said he had in him the making of a great actor. His parodies of other pianists were not always without a sparkle of malice, and his power of sudden alteration of his personality was said by Sand and Liszt to have been remarkable.

"What a jury of pianists," cried Mathias, "in the old palmy days of the Salle Érard! Doehler, Dreyschock, Leopold de Meyer, Zimmerman, Thalberg, Kalkbrenner—how they all curiously examined the Polish black swan, with his original style and extraordinary technique." Chopin ad-mired Weber. Their natures were alike aristocratic. Once, after Mathias had played the chivalric sonata in A flat, Chopin exclaimed: "An angel passes in the sky." Mathias first knew Chopin in 1840 at the Chaussée d'Antin, No. 38. The house no longer stands, having been demolished by the cutting through of the Rue Lafayette. Later he moved to the Rue Tronchet, No. 5. The house is still there—or was when I last saw it ten years ago. Chopin occupied the *rez-de-chaussée*. The first piece of music brought by Mathias at his lesson was by Kalkbrenner and called—oh, horrible!—"Une Pensée de Bellini!" Chopin looked at it, made no comment, for he was diplomatic, and gave the boy the Moscheles Studies and the A minor Concerto of Hummel. When Chopin was sick Fontana gave his master's lessons. One day that Chopin was ill, he received his visitors lying on a couch. Mathias noticed a copy of Schumann's "Carneval." He asked his master what he thought of the strange music, but Chopin answered in icy accents, as if the mere idea of the composition were painful to him. He never spoke well of music in which the form shocked his taste—himself the form-breaker—and so said as little as possible. And poor, devoted Robert Schumann in Germany, pouring out inky rhapsodies over Chopin! Chopin, added Mathias, did not boast the intellectual fibre of Berlioz or Liszt. He was a simple man—"je ne veux pas dire simple esprit." Of the Impromptus, Mathias told me the second and third were his favorites, particularly the second. And he never played twice alike, always making some subtle nuance or slight change in the tempo, or a topsy-turvying of dynamics. Chopin was the chameleon among pianists.

James Huneker

Thematic Index.

IMPROMPTUS.

1.
A♭ Major.

2.
F♯ Major.

3.
G♭ Major.

4.
C♯ Minor.

Impromptu.

F. CHOPIN. Op. 29.

Allegro assai, quasi presto.

Impromptu.

F. CHOPIN. Op. 36.

2.

Andantino.

Impromptu.

à Mme la Comtesse ESTERHÁZY.

F. CHOPIN. Op. 51.

Allegro vivace.

Fantaisie-Impromptu.

(Posthumous.)

F. CHOPIN. Op. 66.

Allegro agitato.

4.

Tempo I.(Allegro agitato.)